The Official
MANCHESTER UNITED
Annual 2014

Written by Steve Bartram & Gemma Thompson

Cover design by Dan James

A Grange Publication

©2013. Published by Grange Communications Ltd., Edinburgh, under licence from Manchester United Football Club. Printed in the EU.

Photography © www.manutdpics.com

ISBN 978-1-908925-46-6

£7.99

CONTENTS

HELLO AND WELCOME TO THE OFFICIAL 2014 MANCHESTER UNITED ANNUAL.

Firstly I have to say how incredibly privileged I feel to be manager of Manchester United. I'll never forget that moment when Sir Alex Ferguson himself told me I would be taking over the job, and I am very grateful to him and the club for making it happen.

Being manager of this great club has already been a fantastic experience, from travelling around the globe on pre-season tour and meeting so many of our fans based in all corners of the world, to winning the first trophy of the season, the Community Shield at Wembley in August. I said at the time that the trophy was for Sir Alex and for the way his team performed last season to win the Barclays Premier League. I very much hope that is something I can experience in the coming seasons and I hope to have the opportunity to lead the team out at Wembley many times in the future – it was certainly an extremely proud moment for me and my family.

Whoever was going to take on this job knows the task at hand – you're following on from an incredible manager, someone who everybody in football around the world looks up to. There is nobody better. All I can do is to keep doing what I have done before. I will continue to honour the traditions of Manchester United but I have to, in my own way, put my own stamp on the club. Sir Alex had to do it when he took over and it took him a little bit of time. I'm very fortunate that I'm taking over the champions of England, and from that point of view, it gives me a great starting point – better than most would ever get.

I've come to a club where the word success is tattooed right across its badge. My job is to continue that. I'm hungry to do it, I'm driven to succeed. The team had a great campaign in the Premier League last season and we'll do everything we can to replicate that this term and to make sure we remain at the top. The support I've had from everybody at the club – the players, the staff and the fans – has been tremendous, and I'm relishing the challenges that lie ahead.

But before we continue to look forward, it's time to look back at the team's fantastic achievements in the league in 2012/13, find out more about our pre-season tour and take part in some quizzes and puzzles that should really test your knowledge of United!

David Moyes

CHANGING OF THE GUARD

On 8 May 2013, the inevitable finally happened. After 26 and a half years, 38 major honours and 1,500 games, Sir Alex Ferguson announced that the 2012/13 campaign would be his final season as Manchester United manager.

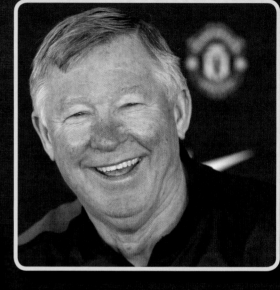

The most successful manager in the history of British football, having just led United to a record-extending 20th league title insisted: "The time is right. I wanted to go out a winner; that was really important."

It was the end to an incredible tale for a man who arrived in Manchester in November 1986 to replace Ron Atkinson, finding a team struggling near the relegation zone and a club with poor scouting networks and youth development.

The latter in particular had been one of United's great strengths, dating back to the days of Sir Matt Busby, and Ferguson quickly set about addressing the drop in standards. While it took three full seasons to bring silverware back to Old Trafford – beating Crystal Palace in the 1990 FA Cup final after a replay – it was the work behind the scenes at the club's Cliff training ground which would pay the biggest dividends.

Glory followed in the European Cup Winners' Cup and League Cup over the following two seasons, but it was United's sustained shortcomings in the league which proved most frustrating. Then, when the First Division evolved into the Premier League at the commencement of the 1992/93 season, came the end of a 26-year wait as United saw off the challenge of Aston Villa to be crowned champions.

That success brought the eighth title of United's history, still lagging English record holders Liverpool by ten titles. Over the ensuing two decades, however, Ferguson would gradually reel in the Merseysiders and he ultimately admitted that his greatest success at Old Trafford was "knocking Liverpool off their perch."

But triumphs weren't just confined to the league. In addition to five FA Cups, four League Cups and ten Community Shields, Ferguson guided his club to the peak of European and World football, twice winning the UEFA Champions League as well as the Intercontinental Cup and Club World Cup.

The Reds' Champions League success of 1999 completed an incredible Treble haul alongside the Premier League and FA Cup, and also prompted the United manager to receive a knighthood and become known as Sir Alex Ferguson. By the time he retired, Old Trafford's North Stand was renamed in Sir Alex's honour and a bronze statue erected in his image.

finest football manager that's ever lived. If I can even win a quarter of what he won I'll have done very well. The first thing is to settle in to the job, get to know everybody and find my own way around."

Moyes is under no illusions as to the size of the job at hand, but, having been hand-picked to replace Britain's greatest ever manager by the man himself, he tackles the task with an almighty vote of confidence.

It was only fitting, then, that he should help choose his successor, and so it transpired when he selected Everton's David Moyes to replace him. None were as shocked as Moyes himself when Sir Alex broke the news.

"It was a really strange situation for me," admits the new United manager. "I had no idea whatsoever. A lot of people thought I'd known something about the job but I knew nothing at all about it until Sir Alex gave me a call and asked me to come to his house. I was expecting him to say, 'I'm going to take one of your players' or something else but we went in and the first thing he said to me was that he was retiring. I said, 'Yeah, when?' He was never retiring, was he? He said 'Next week' and his next words were, 'and you're the next Manchester United manager'."

"I didn't get a chance to say yes or no. I was told I was the next Manchester United manager by Sir Alex. For me, that was enough. As you can imagine, the blood drained from my face. I was shocked that he had chosen to retire but, inside, I was incredibly thrilled that I was going to be given the opportunity to manage Manchester United."

And so it came to pass. Moyes officially began work at the Aon Training Complex on 1 July 2013 and was soon jetting off on the club's pre-season tour. While adjusting to life at a club of United's size will take time, Moyes insists that it must not cloud United's ambitions.

"The objectives for the season are probably no different from what any Manchester United objectives would be: to win as many trophies as possible," he said. "It's my first season as manager and I'm following probably the

SEASON REVIEW
2012/13

AUGUST

Defensive injuries decimated Sir Alex Ferguson's squad ahead of the season opener at Everton, where Michael Carrick was forced to partner the returning Nemanja Vidic at Goodison Park. Marouane Fellaini's header gave the Toffees three points, as even a late cameo for debutant Robin van Persie couldn't turn the tide for United. The Dutchman's influence soon began to tell, however, and he cracked home a stunning goal against Fulham at Old Trafford, as the Reds recovered from Damien Duff's early opener to take the spoils through strikes by van Persie, Shinji Kagawa and Rafael. Coming from behind would emerge as a theme for United during the early weeks of the campaign.

Player of the Month:
Shinji Kagawa

Kagawa confirmed his status as a mouth-watering prospect with two livewire displays, and the Japanese schemer capped his lively outings with a goal against Fulham on his home debut.

Goal of the Month:
Robin van Persie v Fulham

Van Persie's strike against the Cottagers quickly showcased the new boy's capabilities. Patrice Evra's low cross bounced and skidded just in front of the Dutchman, who hooked an outrageous first-time finish over Mark Schwarzer.

Results

20th Premier League – Everton 1 United 0
25th Premier League – United 3 Fulham 2

Sounding off

"Obviously it's not ideal to lose your first game, but none of the players were getting carried away so soon. We knew we would react well." **Danny Welbeck**

Goal of the Month:
Rafael v Liverpool

Few United right-backs have scored at Anfield – fewer still have done so in such spectacular fashion. Taking Shinji Kagawa's chested pass, the Brazilian curled a magnificent left-footed effort into Pepe Reina's top corner to tee up a comeback victory.

Player of the Month:
Rafael

The Brazilian youngster thrived as a regular in the United defence, catching the eye with his proactive, robust style of defending and his increasing threat in attack – as he demonstrated spectacularly against Liverpool.

Results

2nd	Premier League – Southampton 2 United 3
15th	Premier League – United 4 Wigan 0
19th	Champions League – United 1 Galatasaray 0
23rd	Premier League – Liverpool 1 United 2
26th	Capital One Cup 3rd round – United 2 Newcastle 1
29th	Premier League – United 2 Tottenham 3

Sounding off

"It was a great feeling to finally win again at Anfield. Games there are one hundred miles an hour and you don't really understand that until you're out there." **Jonny Evans**

SEPTEMBER

The tone was set for a topsy-turvy month in a rollercoaster trip to promoted Southampton. The Reds fell behind, levelled through Robin van Persie and then conceded again, and van Persie's penalty miss looked set to compound defeat. The Dutchman struck a close-range equaliser, however, and then headed in an injury-time winner to send the travelling fans wild. That preceded a 4-0 stroll against Wigan Athletic and a narrow Champions League win over Galatasaray, before another comeback was required to win at Anfield for the first time in five seasons. Though Newcastle were beaten in the Reds' first Capital One Cup tie of the season, the month ended on a low note when Spurs registered their first Premier League win at Old Trafford.

OCTOBER

A challenging month began with the Champions League trip to Romania, where Robin van Persie's double overcame Cluj, but the Reds' new signing played the role of provider as unlikely goalscorers Jonny Evans, Patrice Evra and Tom Cleverley found the net in a comprehensive win at Newcastle. A hard-fought win over Stoke City preceded another comeback victory over Braga in Europe. Next came a pair of goal-laden trips to face Chelsea at Stamford Bridge, where the early-season pacesetters were beaten by Chicharito's controversial late strike in a five-goal Premier League thriller. The Blues then exacted a degree of revenge as the month drew to a close, beating a youthful Reds side 5-4 after extra time to end United's interest in the Capital One Cup.

Results

2nd   Champions League – Cluj 1 United 2
7th   Premier League – Newcastle 0 United 3
20th   Premier League – United 4 Stoke 2
23rd   Champions League – United 3 Braga 2
28th   Premier League – Chelsea 2 United 3
31st   Capital One Cup 4th round – Chelsea 5
       United 4 AET

Player of the Month: Chicharito

Chicharito's campaign burst into life with a magnificent display against Braga, and he followed that with two more goalscoring displays at Chelsea as his continued to torment the Blues with his unerring finishing.

Goal of the Month: Tom Cleverley v Newcastle

Having opened his United account with a well-taken finish against the Magpies in September, Cleverley went one better with a sublime curling effort from the left flank at St James' Park. He insists it was deliberate, and who are we to doubt him?

Sounding off

"Conceding early goals is a bad habit, but the positive thing is we can say we have shown a good reaction to it."
Patrice Evra

NOVEMBER

United hit the top of the Premier League table for the first time and wrapped up qualification for the knockout stages of the Champions League with two group games to spare. Robin van Persie haunted his former side, Arsenal, with the opening goal in a comfortable victory over the Gunners, then came off the bench to inspire a come-from-behind triumph in Braga to secure progress. Chicharito had a similar impact at Aston Villa, scoring twice and prompting a Ron Vlaar own-goal as United recovered from two goals down to win. There was no such luck at Norwich or Galatasaray, but the month ended on a high with successive home league wins over struggling QPR (who briefly led at a stunned Old Trafford) and West Ham.

Player of the Month: Chicharito

Having hit his stride in October, the Mexican continued that fine vein of form into November, making a game-changing impact at Villa Park and also scoring in victories over Braga and QPR.

Goal of the Month: Chicharito v QPR

Chicharito scored it, but November's outstan goal owed much to the industry of Anderson Brazilian gained possession inside his own ha surged past a posse of defenders before teein his Mexican team-mate for a clinical finish.

Results

3rd   Premier League – United 2 Arsenal 1
7th   Champions League – Braga 1 United 3
10th Premier League – Aston Villa 2 United 3
17th Premier League – Norwich 1 United 0
20th Champions League – Galatasaray 1 United 0
24th Premier League – United 3 QPR 1
28th Premier League – United 1 West Ham 0

Sounding off

"In the history of Manchester United, we never give up until the end. The game is for 90 minutes and you need to play until the last minute." **Chicharito**

DECEMBER

This was the month when United's title charge really gathered momentum. After opening it with a see-saw, madcap win at Reading in which all seven goals were scored in the first half, the Reds rounded off the Champions League group stages with a rare home defeat to Cluj. Then came the most important result of the season: victory in the Manchester derby, where Robin van Persie's injury-time free-kick followed Wayne Rooney's brace to secure an unforgettable away win. A hectic Christmas period yielded wins over Sunderland, Newcastle (yet another comeback completed in injury-time) and West Brom, plus a draw at Swansea, while reigning champions City continued to stutter and allowed United a seven-point lead by the end of 2012.

Player of the Month:
Robin van Persie

No contest. Six appearances brought five vital goals, including what turned out to be the winner at Reading and his last-gasp free-kick at City ensured the Blues' first home league defeat in almost two years.

Goal of the Month:
Wayne Rooney (second)
v Manchester City

A superb, incisive goal borne of United's fine counter-attacking play at the Etihad Stadium. After the ball was patiently worked wide to Rafael, the Brazilian's low cross was clinically swept home by the onrushing Rooney to tee up an invaluable victory.

Results

1st	Premier League – Reading 3 United 4
5th	Champions League – United 0 Cluj 1
9th	Premier League – Man City 2 United 3
15th	Premier League – United 3 Sunderland 1
23rd	Premier League – Swansea 1 United 1
26th	Premier League – United 4 Newcastle 3
29th	Premier League – United 2 West Brom 0

Sounding off

"Christmas is the time to get down to business. Usually when the stakes are high and the concentration is there, good players produce the goods." **Ryan Giggs**

Player of the Month:
Robin van Persie

The Dutchman's superb form showed no signs of slowing, after another goal-laden month. Four in four Premier League starts, plus a vital, last-gasp equaliser at West Ham to keep United in the FA Cup.

JANUARY 2013

New year, same targets. With a handsome lead at the head of the table, Sir Alex merely demanded more of the same from his players to finish the Premier League title race off. Early signs were promising, with Robin van Persie and Chicharito bagging a pair apiece at Wigan. Two attempts were required to oust West Ham from the FA Cup third round, with those ties sandwiching a hard-fought home win over Liverpool, in which van Persie and Nemanja Vidic scored. A last-gasp equaliser from Clint Dempsey held the Reds at Tottenham, before Fulham were steamrollered in the FA Cup fourth round and Southampton were just about navigated in a tough midweek encounter at Old Trafford.

Results

1st   Premier League – Wigan 0 United 4
5th   FA Cup 3rd round – West Ham 2 United 2
13th   Premier League – United 2 Liverpool 1
16th   FA Cup 3rd round replay – United 1 West Ham 0
20th   Premier League – Tottenham 1 United 1
26th   FA Cup 4th round – United 4 Fulham 1
30th   Premier League – United 2 Southampton 1

Sounding off

"I love playing at Old Trafford and I'm always amazed by the atmosphere. The feeling of unity between the supporters and players is incredible." **Shinji Kagawa**

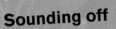

Goal of the Month:
Robin van Persie v West Ham

A goal of beautiful simplicity. From Ryan Giggs' 50-yard pass to van Persie's control, surge and finish, not a single component of the goal was anything less than world class. Phenomenal.

FEBRUARY

The return of the Champions League pitted United against an old friend: Cristiano Ronaldo. Real Madrid's star man loomed large on the horizon, while Manchester City's patchy league form gave the Reds the chance to build an insurmountable points advantage with hard-fought wins over Fulham and Everton. Ryan Giggs scored for the 23rd successive top flight season against the Toffees, and his substitute appearance prompted a rousing reception from the home supporters in United's first-leg trip to Madrid. Inevitably, Ronaldo scored, but only to cancel out Danny Welbeck's opener in an entertaining 1-1 draw which could have ended in victory for either side. After Reading had been eliminated from the FA Cup, Giggs scored again as relegation-threatened QPR were beaten at Loftus Road and the Reds' march to the title continued.

Goal of the Month:
Rafael v QPR

No contest. An absolute thunderbolt from the little Brazilian, who spotted a loose ball bobbling his way and blasted it from fully 25 yards, straight into the top corner of Julio Cesar's goal. Unstoppable.

Results

2nd   Premier League – Fulham 0 United 1
10th Premier League – United 2 Everton 0
13th Champions League last 16, first leg
     – Real Madrid 1 United 1
18th FA Cup 5th round – United 2 Reading 1
23rd Premier League – QPR 0 United 2

Player of the Month:
David De Gea

United's defensive record improved markedly after the turn of the year, owing much to the superb form of De Gea. His displays – in particular a brilliant outing at The Bernabeu – prompted widespread rave reviews.

Sounding off

"We all want to do it together, whether you're starting or a substitute. We all want to work together and win together."
Wayne Rooney

MARCH

While the Reds' relentless pace at the head of the Premier League table showed no signs of slowing, a controversial Champions League exit and FA Cup collapse against Chelsea removed some of the month's gloss. Shinji Kagawa bagged a beautiful hat-trick against Norwich City, before the Reds were sent spinning out of European competition in heart-breaking circumstances. A perfectly executed gameplan had United ahead against Madrid on aggregate through Sergio Ramos' own-goal, only for the baffling dismissal of Nani to turn the tide, and Luka Modric and Cristiano Ronaldo took the Spaniards into the quarter-finals. Though a two-goal lead was blown against Chelsea in the FA Cup, narrow wins over Reading and Sunderland quickly got the season back on track and it was only a matter of time before the 20th league title was confirmed.

Goal of the Month:
Wayne Rooney v Norwich City

Though Shinji Kagawa took the plaudits with a sumptuous hat-trick against the Canaries, Rooney saved the most spectacular goal of the afternoon for last, thumping in a cracking 25-yarder.

Results

2nd   Premier League – United 4 Norwich 0
5th   Champions League last 16, second leg
       – United 1 Real Madrid 2
10th   FA Cup quarter-final – United 2 Chelsea 2
16th   Premier League – United 1 Reading 0
30th   Premier League – Sunderland 0 United 1

Sounding off

"We have reacted well this season. We've trained hard and got into the situation we are in now. We are in charge of the title." **Nemanja Vidic**

Player of the Month:
Michael Carrick

United's midfield lynchpin finally drew long-overdue praise during the course of 2012/13, and it was during a hectic March that he was at the height of his powers, dictating attacking play and shielding his defence admirably.

APRIL

Despite the disappointment of an FA Cup exit to Chelsea and a derby defeat to Manchester City at Old Trafford, a four-point haul from tricky trips to Stoke and West Ham moved United to within touching distance of the title. Robin van Persie had ended a long goalless run with strikes in both games, and the Dutchman bagged a hat-trick – including an incredible volley – against Aston Villa to confirm United's 20th domestic crown with four league games still remaining. Van Persie and his team-mates were afforded a guard of honour by Arsenal on his return to the Emirates Stadium, and United's number 20 cracked home a penalty to quieten his former supporters and ensure a share of the spoils for Sir Alex's side.

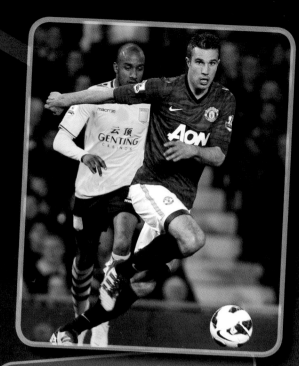

Player of the Month:
Robin van Persie

After a 10-game run without a goal, the Dutchman found his scoring boots again in devastating fashion, hitting six goals in six appearances – including his unforgettable, title-clinching hat-trick against Villa.

Sounding off

"It's a great feeling to win the league. I had to wait a long time. Our new standard is we want to be champions every year and we want to win more. I want to win more." **Robin van Persie**

Results

1st FA Cup quarter-final replay
     – Chelsea 1 United 0
8th Premier League – United 1 Man City 2
14th Premier League – Stoke 0 United 2
17th Premier League – West Ham 2 United 2
22nd Premier League – United 3 Aston Villa 0
28th Premier League – Arsenal 1 United 1

Goal of the Month:
Robin van Persie v Aston Villa

Voted the best goal of the campaign at the club's end of season awards ceremony, the striker's sublime first-time volley from outside the penalty area was the high-point of an exceptional debut campaign at Old Trafford.

MAY

Just when it seemed United were going to coast to another championship coronation without making headlines, Sir Alex Ferguson stunned football with the announcement that he would be retiring from his post after 26 and a half years in charge at Old Trafford. That news followed a lacklustre defeat at home to Chelsea, but preceded an unforgettable farewell against Swansea. Rio Ferdinand's late goal – his first in five years – ensured a winning finish in the boss' final game at Old Trafford, and Sir Alex gave an emotional farewell speech before lifting the Barclays Premier League trophy to an enormous roar from a capacity crowd. His reign ended on a madcap note with a 5-5 draw at West Brom on the final day, before he took his richly-deserved bow in front of the adoring away support at The Hawthorns.

Results

5th   Premier League – United 0 Chelsea 1
12th   Premier League – United 2 Swansea 1
19th   Premier League – West Brom 5 United 5

Player of the Month:
Shinji Kagawa

The Japanese attacker ended the season just as he started it: in eye-catching form. Though he didn't appear in the defeat to Chelsea, his impressive outings against Swansea and West Brom augur well for the future.

Sounding off

"We've thanked the manager for everything he's done and he's thanked us. There is a new challenge ahead for all of us to look forward to."
Michael Carrick

Goal of the Month:
Rio Ferdinand v Swansea City

The sentimental vote wins it. Though the Reds scored a handful of more impressive goals at West Brom, Rio's thunderous late finish against Swansea ensured a winning climax in Sir Alex's Old Trafford finale.

CHAMPIONS

20|13

CHAMPIONS
20|13

PLAYER PROFILES

GOALKEEPERS

1. DAVID DE GEA

Born: 7 November 1990; Madrid, Spain

Previous clubs: Atletico Madrid

Joined United: 1 July 2011

United debut: 7 August 2011 vs Manchester City (N), Community Shield

International team: Spain (youth)

KEY STRENGTHS: The Spanish stopper boasts superb reflexes, pinpoint distribution and an unflappable temperament, and he is regarded as one of the world's best young goalkeepers.

2012/13: After a tough start to life in England during 2011/12, David came of age last term and was one of United's most consistent performers. He was duly recognised by his fellow professionals and named in the PFA Team of the Year.

13. ANDERS LINDEGAARD

Born: 13 April 1984; Dyrup, Denmark

Previous clubs: Odense Boldklub, Kolding FC (loan), Aalesunds FK

Joined United: 4 January 2011

United debut: 29 January 2011 vs Southampton (A), FA Cup

International team: Denmark

KEY STRENGTHS: Composed on the ball, an excellent shot-stopper and a keeper always in command of his penalty area, the Dane is an imposing presence between the sticks.

2012/13: His chances were limited by the excellent form of De Gea, but Lindegaard still played his part in helping the Reds to a 20th league title. He had the honour of being chosen in goal for Sir Alex Ferguson's last-ever game in charge at West Brom.

40. BEN AMOS

Born: 10 April 1990; Macclesfield

Previous clubs: Trainee, Peterborough (loan), Molde (loan), Oldham (loan), Hull City (loan)

Joined United: 1 July 2006

United debut: 23 September 2008 vs Middlesbrough (H), Carling Cup

International team: England (youth)

KEY STRENGTHS: Level-headed with a commanding presence and sharp reflexes, Ben is a keeper of great promise who has represented the club at every level.

2012/13: Ben played his part in helping Championship side Hull City secure automatic promotion to the Premier League after a solid first half of the season on loan with the Tigers. After returning to Old Trafford in January he was a key member of Warren Joyce's triumphant

50. SAM JOHNSTONE

Born: 25 March 1993; Preston

Previous clubs: Trainee, Oldham Athletic (loan), Scunthorpe United (loan), Walsall (loan), Yeovil (loan)

Joined United: 1 July 2009

United debut: N/A

International team: England (youth)

KEY STRENGTHS: Tall, agile and an excellent shot-stopper, Sam has excelled in United's and England's youth ranks. A modest young man with a bright future ahead.

2012/13: Sam spent the opening half of the campaign training with the first team and was on the bench for a couple of League Cup matches and City away in the league. He ended the season in a starring loan role for Walsall with the Saddlers narrowly missing out on reaching the League One play-offs.

DEFENDERS

2. RAFAEL DA SILVA

Born: 9 July 1990; Rio de Janeiro, Brazil

Previous club: Fluminense

Joined United: 1 July 2008

United debut: 17 August 2008 vs Newcastle (H), Premier League

International team: Brazil

KEY STRENGTHS: A bundle of energy who continues to improve defensively and loves to attack, Rafael has developed into one of the finest right-backs in England.

2012/13: After being handed the no.2 shirt at the start of the campaign, Rafael went on to establish himself as United's first choice right-back during what was easily his best season in a red shirt. And he also showed his eye for goal, with two of his three strikes – at Liverpool and QPR – in the running for the club's Goal of the Season award.

3. PATRICE EVRA

Born: 15 May 1981; Dakar, Senegal

Previous clubs: Marsala, Monza, Monaco

Joined United: 10 January 2006

United debut: 14 January 2006 vs Manchester City (A), Premier League

International team: France

KEY STRENGTHS: The energetic defender, who rarely misses a game, is one of the best full-backs in the game and is someone who brings experience, determination and genuine passion to the United cause.

2012/13: Patrice, who continued to captain the Reds when Nemanja Vidic was absent, was once again a mainstay of the back four and not only did he make an important contribution defensively, he enjoyed his best ever season in front of goal, finding the net four times, including what turned out to be the winner at home to Arsenal

4. PHIL JONES

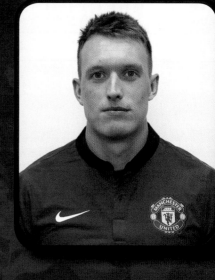

Born: 21 February 1992; Preston

Previous clubs: Blackburn Rovers

Joined United: 1 July 2011

United debut: 7 August 2011 vs Manchester City (N), Community Shield

International team: England

KEY STRENGTHS: A dogged, brave and talented defender who can play at centre-back or full-back and also drop into midfield when needed, he has the potential to become "one of United's greatest ever players," according to former manager Sir Alex Ferguson.

2012/13: Knee surgery prevented Jones from making his first appearance until the end of November, while a bout of tonsillitis and an ankle problem resulted in further spells on the sidelines at times during the campaign. Nonetheless, he more than proved his worth when fit with some all-action displays in defence and, when needed, as extra defensive prowess in midfield.

5. RIO FERDINAND

Born: 7 November 1978; Peckham

Previous clubs: West Ham, Bournemouth (loan), Leeds United

Joined United: 22 July 2002

United debut: 27 August 2002 vs Zalaegerszeg (H), Champions League

International team: England (retired)

KEY STRENGTHS: The highly experienced defender, who announced his retirement from international football in May 2013, oozes calmness, leads by example and possesses an unwavering will to win.

2012/13: Another excellent campaign for Rio who was calmness personified throughout last term. As well as his near-telepathic understanding with Nemanja Vidic, he developed an excellent partnership with Jonny Evans and it was Rio who fired United's late winner – his first goal in five years – against Swansea in Sir Alex's final ever match at Old Trafford. He signed a new one-year contract at the end of the 2012/13 campaign.

6. JONNY EVANS

Born: 3 January 1988; Belfast, Northern Ireland

Previous clubs: Trainee, Royal Antwerp (loan), Sunderland (loan)

Joined United: 1 July 2004

United debut: 26 September 2007 vs Coventry City (H), League Cup

International team: Northern Ireland

KEY STRENGTHS: The United Academy graduate is not only a superb reader of the game, he is a defender with a growing physical presence and confidence who always remains calm under pressure.

2012/13: Jonny was one of the stars of the season and a regular starter in virtually all of the big games. His natural talent and maturity were well complemented by his growing leadership qualities and he made an important contribution at the other end too, finishing the campaign with four goals to his name having only scored once in the previous four-and-a-half years.

12. CHRIS SMALLING

Born: 22 November 1989; Greenwich
Previous clubs: Maidstone United, Fulham
Joined United: 7 July 2010
United debut: 8 August 2010 vs Chelsea (N), Community Shield
International team: England

KEY STRENGTHS: An intelligent, cool customer who can play centrally or at right-back, Chris seems set to become an important performer for both club and country over the coming years.

2012/13: While delighted to be part of another title-winning campaign, the season was ultimately one of frustration for Chris who started and ended the campaign on the treatment table. A fractured metatarsal during pre-season kept him sidelined until November, but he was heavily involved soon after Christmas. Unfortunately though, another injury kept him out of the final seven weeks of the campaign.

15. NEMANJA VIDIC

Born: 21 October 1981; Uzice, Serbia
Previous clubs: Red Star Belgrade, Spartak Subotica (loan), Spartak Moscow
Joined United: 5 January 2006
United debut: 25 January 2006 vs Blackburn Rovers (H), League Cup
International team: Serbia (retired)

KEY STRENGTHS: United's captain is as talented as he is brave and is a huge presence in the Reds' backline. His no-nonsense style is the perfect foil for Rio Ferdinand, with the pair having formed one of the world's best central defensive partnerships.

2012/13: Having endured a lengthy spell on the sidelines the previous term, Vidic was left frustrated once more when just five games into his comeback he found himself back on the operating table for more knee surgery. He returned in December to play his part in another memorable campaign and even chipped in with United's winner at home to Liverpool.

22. FABIO DA SILVA

Born: 9 July 1990; Rio de Janeiro, Brazil
Previous club: Fluminense, QPR (loan)
Joined United: 1 July 2008
United debut: 24 January 2009 vs Tottenham Hotspur (H), FA Cup
International team: Brazil (youth)

KEY STRENGTHS: Injuries have taken their toll in recent years, but, like his brother, his all-action style of play continues to delight fans and his enthusiasm is infectious.

2012/13: In a bid to enhance his first-team experience, he spent the 2012/13 campaign on loan at QPR. The first half of his spell was ultimately punctuated by injuries, but under Harry Redknapp, Fabio grew in confidence after Christmas and featured regularly for Rangers who were relegated to The Championship.

28. ALEXANDER BUTTNER

Born: 11 February 1989; Doetinchem, Netherlands
Previous clubs: VV Doetinchem, Ajax, Vitesse Arnhem
Joined United: 21 August 2012
United debut: 15 September 2012 vs Wigan (H), Premier League
International team: Holland (youth)

KEY STRENGTHS: Signed initially as cover for Patrice Evra, the winger-turned-defender brings energy in defence and attack, and made an instant impact with a fine goal on his United debut.

2012/13: While his chances were limited by the almost ever-present Evra, when given his chance Alex showed glimpses of his potential as an all-action full-back and showed his eye for goal both on his debut against Wigan and in Sir Alex's final game in charge at The Hawthorns.

38. MICHAEL KEANE

Born: 11 January 1993; Stockport
Previous clubs: Trainee, Leicester City (loan)
Joined United: 1 July 2009
United debut: 25 October 2011 vs Aldershot (A), League Cup
International team: England (youth)

KEY STRENGTHS: Started out as a full-back, but has since developed into an accomplished centre-half. He is the twin brother of Reds striker Will and was named the Denzil Haroun Reserve Player of the Year in 2012.

2012/13: Keane began the season at Old Trafford and started both of United's League Cup games against Newcastle and Chelsea, who defeated the Reds in round four. He joined Leicester on loan at the star of November, making 27 appearances and scoring three goals on the way to helping the Foxes reach the Championship play-off semi-finals.

MIDFIELDERS

8. ANDERSON

Born: 13 April 1988; Porto Alegre, Brazil
Previous clubs: Gremio, FC Porto
Joined United: 1 July 2007
United debut: 1 September 2007 vs Sunderland (H), Premier League
International team: Brazil

KEY STRENGTHS: Injuries may have hindered his progress at Old Trafford, but the ever-bubbly and positive Anderson still has the ability to burst forward with the ball and power past defenders.

2012/13: Ando scooped his fourth title winners' medal in six seasons and while his campaign once again included spells in the treatment room, he made his influence count when given his opportunity. And his two goals of the campaign – against Newcastle and Reading –

11. RYAN GIGGS

Born: 29 November 1973; Cardiff, Wales

Previous clubs: Trainee

Joined United: 9 July 1990

United debut: 2 March 1991 vs Everton (H), First Division

International team: Wales (retired)

KEY STRENGTHS: United's record appearance-maker with over 900 games under his belt continues to be an influential presence, whether it be from central midfield or the left wing. Quite simply the most successful player in the history of English football.

2012/13: After captaining Team GB at the 2012 Olympics, British football's most decorated player, who signed a new one-year deal in March 2013, enjoyed another excellent campaign and continued to set yet more records...he racked up his 1,000th competitive game in domestic, international and Olympic football, continued his run of having played and scored in every Premier League season and claimed his 13th championship crown.

16. MICHAEL CARRICK

Born: 28 July 1981; Wallsend

Previous clubs: West Ham, Swindon (loan), Birmingham (loan), Tottenham Hotspur

Joined United: 31 July 2006

United debut: 23 August 2006 vs Charlton Athletic (A), Premier League

International team: England

KEY STRENGTHS: An unassuming player of huge intelligence and calmness, Michael has the ability to control United's – and England's – midfield with his astute range of passing and vision.

2012/13: "His best season for United," declared former boss Sir Alex Ferguson when asked about the man named Players' Player of the Year at Old Trafford and picked for the PFA Team of the Year. The midfielder's campaign rarely dropped below excellence, ensuring a regular starting berth for both club and country and, finally, plaudits from around the football world.

17. NANI

Born: 17 November 1986; Praia, Cape Verde

Previous club: Sporting Lisbon

Joined United: 1 July 2007

United debut: 5 August 2007 vs Chelsea (N), Community Shield

International team: Portugal

KEY STRENGTHS: A two-footed, unpredictable winger with pace and skill aplenty, when he's in the mood Nani is a tough player to stop. Also has the ability to find the target from long range.

2012/13: When at his best Nani is virtually unplayable, but we only saw mere flashes of the winger's bewitching best thanks to formation changes (most notably the diamond) and niggling injuries. Just a month after hitting the 200-game milestone for United he was unjustly sent off against Real Madrid, leaving his and the Reds' Champions League dreams in tatters.

18. ASHLEY YOUNG

Born: 9 July 1985; Stevenage

Previous clubs: Watford, Aston Villa

Joined United: 1 July 2011

United debut: 7 August 2011 vs Manchester City (N), Community Shield

International team: England

KEY STRENGTHS: Fast, skilful and versatile, Young can play on either wing and also in a central role behind the main striker. Offers a real goal threat from distance as well.

2012/13: Young ended the campaign with mixed feelings – frustration at finishing the season on crutches having endured an injury-blighted term, but unconfined joy at securing his first title medal. He was at his best during November and December and while he drew a blank in the goalscoring stakes, he still made a vital contribution when it came to goal-creating.

23. TOM CLEVERLEY

Born: 12 August 1989; Basingstoke

Previous clubs: Trainee, Leicester City (loan), Watford (loan), Wigan (loan)

Joined United: 1 July 2005

United debut: 7 August 2011 vs Manchester City (N), Community Shield

International team: England

KEY STRENGTHS: Having progressed through the ranks at Old Trafford, the gifted midfielder's influence continues to grow for both club and country. An excellent passer of the ball with great vision, he is, according to Sir Alex Ferguson "potentially the best midfielder in Britain."

2012/13: The season was one of real progress for Tom for both club and country and his midfield partnership with Michael Carrick caught the eye. He finally broke his United duck, in front of the Stretford End against Newcastle and netted a further three times – all superb strikes. Collecting his first championship medal has only made him hungrier to improve and achieve more.

24. DARREN FLETCHER

Born: 1 February 1984; Edinburgh, Scotland

Previous clubs: Trainee

Joined United: 3 July 2000

United debut: 12 March 2003 vs FC Basel (H), Champions League

International team: Scotland

KEY STRENGTHS: The man for the big occasion, Fletch is one of the most committed and fittest midfielders you'll find in the game. An intelligent player who reads the game brilliantly, he brings great energy to United's engine room.

2012/13: Having been sidelined by an ulcerative colitis condition since December 2011, the Scot returned to action in September 2012 and made ten appearances up to Christmas, scoring one goal. However, he was forced to miss the remainder of the campaign after surgery to resolve his condition.

25. ANTONIO VALENCIA

Born: 4 August 1985; Lago Agrio, Ecuador
Previous clubs: El Nacional, Villarreal, Recreativo (loan), Wigan
Joined United: 30 June 2009
United debut: 9 August 2009 vs Chelsea (N), Community Shield
International team: Ecuador

KEY STRENGTHS: The Ecuadorian winger, who opted to change his number from 7 to 25 at the start of the 2013/14 campaign, has the pace and power to leave even the world's best defenders trailing in his wake, while his pinpoint deliveries continue to be regularly gobbled up by the United front men.

2012/13: Antonio himself admitted that he did not hit his usual standards during the first part of the season, but he looked much more like his old self during the business end of proceedings and made an important contribution to United's title triumph.

26. SHINJI KAGAWA

Born: 17 March 1989; Kobe, Japan
Previous clubs: FC Miyagi Barcelona, Cerezo Osaka, Borussia Dortmund
Joined United: 1 July 2012
United debut: 20 August 2012 vs Everton (A), Premier League
International: Japan

KEY STRENGTHS: Shinji became United's first ever Japanese player in July 2012 after agreeing a four-year deal. A highly intelligent and technically gifted attacking midfielder, he has the ability to excel in a number of different forward positions.

2012/13: A very encouraging season for the Japanese international who made 26 appearances and found the net six times. After scoring on his home debut against Fulham, his stand-out contribution was his quite brilliant hat-trick – the first for an Asian player in the Premier League – in the 4-0 win over Norwich.

32. NICK POWELL

Born: 23 March 1994; Crewe
Previous clubs: Crewe Alexandra, Wigan (loan)
Joined United: 1 July 2012
United debut: 15 September 2012 vs Wigan (H), Premier League
International: England (youth)

KEY STRENGTHS: The player tipped by Sir Alex to fill the boots of Paul Scholes attracted many top-flight admirers before he joined the Reds. An intelligent attacker with sharp passing skills, Powell has already proved he can smash the ball in from distance too.

2012/13: The young recruit came with a glowing reputation and he certainly made a big impression on his United debut – netting a sublime strike after coming off the bench. Only five more first-team appearances followed thereafter, but in his own words Powell has "grown up on and off the pitch" in just 12 months as a Red.

44. ADNAN JANUZAJ

Born: 5 February 1995; Brussels, Belgium

Previous club: Anderlecht

Joined United: 1 July 2011

United debut: 11 August 2013 vs Wigan (N), Community Shield

KEY STRENGTHS: A highly talented midfielder who has the ability to pull the strings from a central area, create openings from wide areas and cause danger from set-pieces.

2012/13: Played a key role in the Under-21s' Premier League success and was handed the no.44 shirt late on in the campaign. After being named the Denzil Haroun Reserve Team Player of the Year, he was named on the bench for Sir Alex's final game in charge away to West Brom, and he caught the eye and scored during United's 2013 pre-season tour.

STRIKERS

10. WAYNE ROONEY

Born: 24 October 1985; Liverpool

Previous club: Everton

Joined United: 31 August 2004

United debut: 28 September 2004 vs Fenerbahce (H), Champions League

International team: England

KEY STRENGTHS: A key member of the squad who can make the difference in games, Wayne, who has played over 400 games for the Reds, continues to show his quality as a striker and has also proved h can bring much to the side from a deeper role in midfield or either flank

2012/13: Rooney himself described the campaign as "a stop-start season" after niggling injuries and illness forced him out of action at various stages. But he still exerted his huge influence, at times from midfield, as a creator and scorer of important goals, including two of United's three in the dramatic victory at City.

14. JAVIER HERNANDEZ

Born: 1 June 1988; Guadalajara, Mexico

Previous club: Chivas de Guadalajara

Joined United: 1 July 2010

United debut: 8 August 2010 vs Chelsea (N), Community Shield

International team: Mexico

KEY STRENGTHS: An attacking livewire always on the shoulders of defenders, Hernandez has already netted over 50 goals for the Reds in three seasons. Possesses speed, movement and an unerring eye for goal.

2012/13: It was another prolific season for the striker who notched 18 goals in total (second only to RvP), even if a lack of regular starts took the edge off his personal delight. His goals in the memorable wins at home to Newcastle and away to Chelsea and Villa were key

19. DANNY WELBECK

Born: 26 November 1990; Manchester

Previous clubs: Trainee, Preston North End (loan), Sunderland (loan)

Joined United: 1 July 2007

United debut: 23 September 2008 vs Middlesbrough (H), League Cup

International team: England

KEY STRENGTHS: The Manchester-born striker, who has played for the Reds since the age of eight, is always full of running and endeavour and is blessed with superb skill and hustle.

2012/13: A regular starter in the big games and an important member of the squad, Danny could always be relied upon to put in a good shift whether up front or on the wing, even if his return of just two goals for the campaign set him a clear area for improvement this term and beyond.

20. ROBIN VAN PERSIE

Born: 6 August 1983; Rotterdam, Netherlands

Previous clubs: Feyenoord, Arsenal

Joined United: 17 August 2012

United debut: 20 August 2012 vs Everton (A), Premier League

International team: Netherlands

KEY STRENGTHS: One of the best strikers the Premier League has ever seen, Robin has skill, intelligence and finishing ability aplenty. And not only is he adept at finding the net, he's equally deadly in setting up others, particularly from set-pieces.

2012/13: Things could not have gone any better for Robin in his debut season for the Reds. A goal on his home debut, a last-minute derby winner, 30 goals in total, a host of personal accolades, including the Sir Matt Busby Player of the Year, Goal of the Season and Golden Boot prizes, and most importantly a championship medal.

21. ANGELO HENRIQUEZ

Born: 13 April 1994; Santiago, Chile

Previous clubs: Universidad de Chile, Wigan (loan), Real Zaragoza (loan)

Joined United: 5 September 2012

United debut: N/A

International team: Chile

KEY STRENGTHS: A penalty box poacher with great pace who has been compared with former Red Ruud van Nistelrooy. United had watched Angelo for a while before interest from elsewhere prompted the Reds to make their move.

2012/13: After completing his move to Old Trafford in the summer of 2012, the Chilean international found first-team opportunities hard to come by. In a bid to enhance his top-level experience he joined Wigan on loan from January to May but only featured eight times, scoring once.

Old Trafford Arrivals

Sir Alex Ferguson always said that when he left his post as United manager, he would leave the club in a healthy position on and off the pitch, and he stayed true to his word. With youth – as ever – very much at the forefront of his thinking, he ensured David Moyes began his reign at Old Trafford with two exciting additions to the squad. The acquisition of Crystal Palace's Wilfried Zaha, one of the country's most sought-after young talents, was sealed in January 2013 and he spent five months on loan at Selhurst Park before joining up with the Reds. The first official signing of the post-Sir Alex era, meanwhile, was Uruguayan full-back Guillermo Varela, enlisted after impressing on a short-term trial with the champions. And then just minutes before the transfer window slammed shut, the Reds managed to secure the services of Everton's Belgian midfielder Marouane Fellaini.

Here, we bring you the lowdown on United's three new recruits...

29. WILFRIED ZAHA

Born: 10 November 1992; Abidjan, Ivory Coast
Previous club: Crystal Palace
Joined United: 1 July 2013
International team: England

KEY STRENGTHS: A highly skilled winger in possession of pace, intelligence and tricks aplenty. Has the ability to find the net from long range and has an excellent eye for goal in and around the box.

PROFILE: Wilfried Zaha arrived at Old Trafford with a glowing reputation and he has continued to enhance it since officially becoming a Red on 1 July 2013. The winger's capture from Crystal Palace was initially announced in January 2013. He remained at Selhurst Park on loan for the remainder of the campaign and not only helped the Eagles secure promotion to the Barclays Premier League, he picked up the Championship Player of the Year prize following a scintillating campaign.

It's hard to believe Zaha only made his first-team debut at senior level in March 2010 as a 17-year-old. The then Eagles caretaker boss Paul Hart handed the winger a 10-minute cameo against Cardiff, before he was offered a professional contract a month later. The 2010/11 campaign resulted in 44 appearances and Palace's Young Player of the Year award, an accolade he also claimed the following season.

The England international, who was given his first cap by Roy Hodgson in November 2012 in a friendly defeat to Sweden, caught the eye in Palace's shock 2-1 League Cup win at Old Trafford in November 2011, and just over a year later it was announced that the Theatre of Dreams would become his permanent home. He has the potential to be a vital weapon in United's attacking armoury over the coming seasons.

"Being a Manchester United player is an amazing feeling. I was awestruck when I first came, but just being around the other players makes me realise they are all down-to-earth guys and just like me really. My target for this season is just to do my best, get some minutes on the clock and help the team be successful." *Wilfried Zaha*

34

30. GUILLERMO VARELA

Born: 24 March 1993; Montevideo, Uruguay
Previous club: Club Atletico Penarol
Joined United: 11 June 2013
International team: Uruguay (youth)

KEY STRENGTHS: The right-sided full-back is very aware of his defensive responsibilities, while offering plenty as an attacking asset. A player with good pace, he is also an excellent crosser of the ball.

PROFILE: Guillermo Varela earned his position as a Red after completing a successful trial with the club last term. He spent the entirety of his short stay in Manchester training exclusively with the first team and impressed throughout.

The right-back was officially unveiled after Sir Alex's departure in June 2013, but the former boss gave the Uruguayan youth international a glowing endorsement during discussions with new boss David Moyes.

Varela, who quickly developed a close friendship with Chicharito and United's other South American stars, joined from hometown club Club Atletico Penarol. He starred for Uruguay at the FIFA Under-20 World Cup in Turkey in the summer of 2013 and helped his country finish the tournament as runners-up. And he soon made a bright start to life at United with Warren Joyce's Under-21s.

Brimming with potential but with much to learn, Guillermo is a rough diamond in the Reds' defensive ranks, but he provides exciting cover in Moyes' right-back area.

31. MAROUANE FELLAINI

Born: 22 November 1987; Etterbeek, Belgium
Previous clubs: Anderlecht, Mons, R. Francs Borains, Sporting Charleroi, Standard Liege, Everton
Joined United: 2 September 2013
International team: Belgium

KEY STRENGTHS: A real handful for defenders, the Belgian midfielder is brave and talented, and an extremely determined character with a real eye for goal. While posing a threat in attack, his height and physique means he's also a very useful defensive weapon at set-pieces.

PROFILE: On a frantic transfer deadline day, the Reds completed the signing of Everton midfielder Marouane Fellaini right at the death on 2 September, 2013.

The Belgian midfielder declared his move to Old Trafford "something that every player dreams of," having established himself as one of the Premier League's leading midfielders and an international regular during half a decade in England.

Fellaini arrived at Everton in 2008 from Belgium's Standard Liege. The big-haired attacker caught the eye throughout his five years on Merseyside, making 173 appearances and netting 32 goals, a sufficient return to persuade former manager David Moyes to make the midfielder his first major signing at United.

RED ROBIN!

10

Robin van Persie's debut campaign at Manchester United could hardly have gone better. The deadly Dutchman plundered 30 goals in his maiden season at Old Trafford, leading the Barclays Premier League scoring charts and bagging a championship medal at the first time of asking. In celebration of Robin's memorable contribution to our 20th title, we relive the top 10 goals of his 2012/13 season...

10. TOTTENHAM HOTSPUR 1 UNITED 1

At a snow-swept White Hart Lane, Robin made a mockery of the conditions and an unforgiving angle by putting United ahead in clinical style. Tom Cleverley's deep cross was superb, but the back-pedalling Dutchman still had to pull off a magnificent header to bullet a finish inside Hugo Lloris' near post.

9. CHELSEA 2 UNITED 3

"I love playing against Chelsea and I've scored all my goals against them at Stamford Bridge. It's a great place to play, and win," says Robin. A simple finish on this occasion, blasting home a right-footed effort from close-range, but the Reds' approach play, culminating in Antonio Valencia's drilled cross, was superb.

9

8. BRAGA 1 UNITED 3

Having toiled for almost 80 minutes without threatening the Portuguese side, United finally drew level when substitute van Persie latched onto Ryan Giggs' pass and spotted goalkeeper Beto charging from his line. Though the goalkeeper changed his mind and turned back, it was too late and he was beaten by a supreme long-range shot.

7. MANCHESTER CITY 2 UNITED 3

The most important goal of Robin's first season at United. Tied at 2-2 going into injury-time, United won a free-kick, 25 yards from Joe Hart's goal. "Wayne Rooney and I discussed what to do at the free-kick," says van Persie. "Shoot or cross? My shot deflected off the wall past Hart. You can't get luckier than that!"

6. CLUJ 1 UNITED 2

For all his raw power, it was Robin's deftness which caught the eye in Romania. Wayne Rooney's chipped pass over the Cluj defence arced perfectly into the striker's path, and he gently nudged a measured finish past the onrushing goalkeeper. "It was a fantastic Wazza pass," says Robin. "And the ball spun into the net beautifully."

5

5. UNITED 2 WEST BROM 0

For much of a tense afternoon, United struggled to see off the spirited challenge of Steve Clarke's Baggies. Thrown into the fray as a substitute, Robin settled matters with a blistering finish, receiving the ball in the visitors' area, meandering across the box to make space and cracking a curling effort high over Ben Foster.

4

4. WIGAN ATHLETIC 0 UNITED 4

Both Robin and Chicharito scored twice, but the Dutchman's first goal stole the show. "It was a good goal because every single touch was the right touch," says van Persie, who shaped to shoot with his left foot, dragged the ball back onto his right and curled home a fabulous finish. As he says: "Three touches but all good touches."

3. UNITED 3 FULHAM 2

"It was a dream start, scoring after 10 minutes of my home debut. What a day," says Robin. Better still that he opened his United account in spectacular fashion. As Patrice Evra's drilled cross came into the box, van Persie peeled away from Brede Hangeland and hooked an unstoppable volley across Mark Schwarzer to send Old Trafford into raptures.

3

2. WEST HAM 2 UNITED 2

United looked to be heading out of the FA Cup at the first hurdle, only for a goal of staggering brilliance to secure a replay against the Hammers. "Giggsy's pass was unbelievable. I didn't break stride," says Robin, of his team-mate's sublime 50-yard pass. Of his own excellence, he understates: "I had a good first touch and a decent finish."

1. UNITED 3 ASTON VILLA 0

The perfect way to seal the title. Wayne Rooney picked up the ball in midfield and immediately looked for his strike partner, before picking him out with a stunning chipped pass. "I looked up and thought: 'This ball is so nice. It's too beautiful to take a touch'," says van Persie, who thundered home a perfect volleyed finish to further underline his unquestioned class.

THE COMEBACK KINGS

United's 2012/13 title triumph was built on the club's nerve-shredding tradition of winning after falling behind.

Here are the top five Reds comebacks from the Premier League era...

5. City 2 United 3,
7 November 1993

One of the most satisfying victories the Reds have ever enjoyed in the Premier League era. Fresh from exiting the Champions League against Galatasaray, United's players and fans were subjected to sustained ribbing from City supporters – even before the hosts had roared into a two-goal lead through Niall Quinn's pair of headers. No matter, Eric Cantona merely picked up the baton and set about conducting United's response. The Frenchman pounced on a Michel Vonk mistake and halved the deficit, then restored parity by tapping home Ryan Giggs' sublime back-post pass. As time ticked away and both sides pushed for the win, United pinched the points when Roy Keane smashed in Denis Irwin's cross to silence the home support once and for all.

4. West Ham 2 United 4,
2 April 2011

Another fightback reserved for a nerve-jangling title run-in. Two Mark Noble penalties put West Ham ahead and in a position of comfort which they retained until 25 minutes from the end. United had been desperately poor all afternoon at Upton Park and looked set to drop vital points, until Wayne Rooney burst into life and curled home a superb free-kick. That goal provided the spark for another trademark comeback victory, with Rooney powering home a clinical equaliser and converting a late penalty. Such was the game's dramatic shift in momentum that there was still time for Chicharito to round off the scoring with a close-range tap-in six minutes before the end.

3. Everton 2 United 4,
28 April 2007

Nerves appeared to be gripping Sir Alex Ferguson's men as they sought to bring the Premier League title back to Old Trafford for the first time in four seasons. Alan Stubbs' deflected free-kick had David Moyes' men ahead by the break, and Manuel Fernandes thundered home a second goal after 50 minutes. United's poor display never hinted at what would follow. Sparked by a goalkeeping error which allowed John O'Shea to rifle home from close-range, the Reds levelled through a Phil Neville own goal and moved into the lead for the first time with 11 minutes remaining thanks to Wayne Rooney's cool finish. When rookie winger Chris Eagles sealed victory in injury-time with a fine solo goal, United were within touching distance of getting the trophy back.

2. United 5 Tottenham 2,
25 April 2009

Poor Spurs. Once again, the Londoners roared into a two-goal half-time lead, only to succumb to another incredible United comeback. This time, the Reds only needed to hit form for a devastating 22-minute period which housed five goals, though the first came with an element of good fortune as Cristiano Ronaldo converted an incorrectly-awarded penalty. Once the Portuguese international had struck, however, there was no stopping the hosts, who went from trailing to leading in the space of 11 minutes as Wayne Rooney netted United's second, then crossed for a fine Ronaldo header. To rub salt in Spurs' wounds, Rooney and Dimitar Berbatov both squeezed home close-range finishes to put United on the brink of an 18th league title.

1. Tottenham 3 United 5,
29 September 2001

The definitive game of two halves. United were awful throughout the first period, rarely threatening in attack and conceding three sloppy goals to the rampant hosts. After the break, however, followed one of the greatest 45-minute displays in the club's history. Andy Cole converted a diving header in the first minute of the second period, and from then on Tottenham's players and fans appeared frozen in fear. Laurent Blanc and Ruud van Nistelrooy scored headers to haul the Reds level, before Juan Sebastian Veron drilled a fabulous low shot past Neil Sullivan to completely overturn the match with 14 minutes remaining. Captain David Beckham then powered home United's fifth and final goal in the 87th minute

REDS
IN TRAINING

FAREWELL to the MASTER

He reneged on retirement once, but Paul Scholes irreversibly brought down the curtain on his stellar career at the end of last season. One of English football's most decorated players rarely hogged the limelight or the headlines, but he certainly made an impression on those who played with or against him. We give you Scholesy, in the words of his peers…

"I've always wanted to play like Paul Scholes. I've been watching him on television for years and always learned from him." **Andres Iniesta**

"Playing with Paul was a privilege. He made football look easy, which is a difficult thing to do."
Wayne Rooney

"For any football player in the Premier League, Scholes is a player you want to emulate."
Cesc Fabregas

"Paul Scholes is one of the most complete footballers I've ever seen. Of all the English players, I've always liked his style of play the most."
Xavi

"When I get asked who's the greatest player you've played with I struggle to pick just one, but Scholesy is up there and I've always said he's probably my favourite because he could do things that no other player could."
Ryan Giggs

"I have no hesitation in putting a name to the embodiment of all that I think is best about football. It's Paul Scholes. Many great players have worn the shirt of Manchester United. Players I worshipped, then lost with my youth in Munich. Players like Denis Law and George Best who I enjoyed so much as team-mates and more recently the players I have watched closely in the Alex Ferguson era. And in so many ways Scholes is my favourite." **Sir Bobby Charlton**

"The first team used to go and watch the youth team play, and Scholesy was one of those young players who made you go 'wow'. The first time you saw him play, you knew this kid was going to be a big player."
Peter Schmeichel

"For me, Scholes is like a teacher. He's the best I've seen play, the best player Manchester United have had."
Anderson

"Scholesy was just a coach's perfect player. He could do everything and he was a great professional with it; one of the very best I've had the pleasure to work with. He really was one of a kind." **Steve McClaren**

"Scholesy was one of the most intelligent players I played with in my career. When you're a striker playing in front of him, he makes life easy for you. You make a run and before you know it you've got the ball in your stride and all you have to worry about is the finish." **Teddy Sheringham**

The LEGENDS Return

Charity was the big winner at the Manchester United Foundation's Red Heart United music and football extravaganza at Old Trafford.

Managed by former captain and club ambassador Bryan Robson, a team of United legends and their Real Madrid counterparts did battle at the Theatre of Dreams after a star-studded concert, which included performances from X Factor stars Amelia Lily and boyband JLS, and United fan and rapper Tinchy Stryder.

A host of former Reds favourites, including Paul Scholes, Jaap Stam and Andy Cole, returned to Old Trafford for the match, the second instalment of a two-legged tie following Real's victory in Madrid in the summer of 2012.

Madrid, who had the likes of Luis Figo, Zinedine Zidane and Claude Makelele in their squad, had run out 3-2 winners in Spain, and the visitors increased their advantage just before half-time at Old Trafford when Fernando Morientes finally found a way past the inspired Edwin van der Sar.

Ruud van Nistelrooy – who played a half each for his two former clubs, the first for Real and the second for United – gave the Reds a lifeline not long after the hour-mark with a sublime finish into the roof of the net, before Ruben de la Red made sure of a 5-3 aggregate victory for Real with a craftily dinked finish over substitute goalkeeper Raimond van der Gouw.

Over £800,000 was raised from the event which was attended by over 60,000 fans, including Sir Alex Ferguson, who got into the party spirit by joining in a stadium-wide Mexican wave. Those substantial funds generated – which went towards supporting the Foundation's many projects in the local area – ensured that, despite the result, the afternoon provided plentiful cause for celebration.

The fans were magnificent and they really made the occasion special. We had some truly great players on show and some great entertainment, but it was the fans who made everything possible. It's a shame we couldn't deliver the result all the United fans were hoping for but the Foundation was the real winner.

It was a fantastic day out for the fans and a great event to be part of. It's always good to see some old faces and there is still no better feeling than playing at Old Trafford.

2 JUNE 2013, RED HEART UNITED, OLD TRAFFORD

UNITED LEGENDS 1
(van Nistelrooy 68)

REAL MADRID LEGENDS 2
(Morientes 39, de la Red 85)

Madrid win 5-3 on aggregate

United: Van der Sar (van der Gouw 70); Berg (Martin 9), Stam, Johnsen, Irwin; Blackmore (van Nistelrooy 46), Fortune, Scholes, Sharpe (Thornley 51, Blomqvist 87); Yorke, Cole.

Real Madrid: Contreras (Sanchez 62); Salgado (Pavon 69), Helguera, Pavon (McManaman 46), Amavisca; Figo (Vazquez 78), Hierro, Makelele (Sanz 62), Zidane; Morientes, van Nistelrooy (de la Red 46).

I was very grateful for the reception I got. For me, it meant a lot to come back to Old Trafford and step out on the pitch. I was even lucky enough to score in front of the Stretford End again!

RUUD VAN NISTELROOY

JETSET REDS

Every summer the team jet off across the world to begin preparations for the new season and to see their many fans who reside in all corners of the globe.

The Reds' pre-season preparations in 2013 were no different with David Moyes' men travelling to Thailand, Australia, Japan, Hong Kong and Sweden during July and August as part of Tour 2013 presented by Aon. For the players, much of the trip was spent working hard on the training pitch preparing for six tour matches, but there was also time for a bit of rest and relaxation during the team's busy schedule…

BANGKOK

First stop on tour was the capital of Thailand…

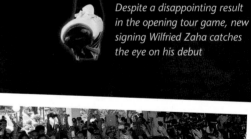

Jonny Evans and Rafael take time out to offer advice to local youngsters at a Nike event

Despite a disappointing result in the opening tour game, new signing Wilfried Zaha catches the eye on his debut

"The reaction we get in Asia is always amazing. It reminds you how many fans we have all over the world when you visit places like this. Their knowledge and passion for the club is fantastic."

Jonny Evans

Match stats
Singha 80th Anniversary Cup, Saturday 13 July 2013
Rajamangala Stadium, Bangkok
SINGHA ALL STAR XI 1 (Winothai 50)
MANCHESTER UNITED 0

Incredible scenes as David Moyes, Ryan Giggs and senior club officials arrive to honour the King of Thailand

SYDNEY

A week in Oz allowed the team to do some intense work on the training pitch...

Ferdinand, Carrick, Moyes and Giggs pose in front of the famous Sydney Opera House

Patrice Evra comes face-to-face with a koala bear at Taronga Zoo

Match stats
Saturday 20 July 2013
ANZ Stadium, Sydney
FOXTEL A-LEAGUE ALL STARS 1 (Berisha 52)
MANCHESTER UNITED 5 (Lingard 11, 55; Welbeck 34, 70; van Persie 87)

"Pre-season is all about fitness and we all worked very hard on tour. Our week in Sydney was very productive. The facilities were great and it's a very nice country. And we have fantastic fans over there."

Rafael

Jesse Lingard and Danny Welbeck fire two goals apiece in 5-1 win for Reds over the A-League All Stars

An alternative training location for the squad on Bondi Beach

David Moyes meets Shinji for the first time as the pair address the media at a press conference

YOKOHAMA

The Reds made a flying visit to the city where they were crowned world champions in 2008...

Match stats
Kagome Re:Generation Challenge, Tuesday 23 July 2013
Nissan Stadium, Yokohama
YOKOHAMA F·MARINOS 3 (Marquinhos 1, Aguiar 49, Fujita 87)
MANCHESTER UNITED 2 (Lingard 19, Tashiro (OG) 31)

Despite another goal from Lingard, the Reds lost out late on to the Marinos

OSAKA

A match against Shinji Kagawa's old team followed...

Match stats
Yanmar Premium Cup, Friday 26 July 2013
Nagai Stadium, Osaka
CEREZO OSAKA 2 (Sugimoto 34, Minamino 63)
MANCHESTER UNITED 2 (Kagawa 54, Zaha 90)

"We're all working very hard to get fit and in my opinion, given the way we train and the way I have got to know the guys over the last year, I'm certain we can win more trophies." **Robin van Persie**

Japanese warriors await the players' arrival at Osaka Castle for the away kit launch

The players board the bullet train to Osaka

Fans in Japan got what they wanted on matchday – a goal from Shinji during the 2-2 draw with his former team

HONG KONG

The team made a first return to HK since 2005...

Despite concerns over the pitch after torrential rain, the Reds run out comfortable winners against Kitchee

Match stats
Monday 29 July 2013
Hong Kong Stadium, Hong Kong
KITCHEE 2 (Lam 53, Alex 69)
MANCHESTER UNITED 5 (Welbeck 16, Smalling 22, Fabio 26, Januzaj 50, Lingard 80)

Adnan Januzaj and Jesse Lingard enjoy a game of dodgeball with local youngsters who are being helped by UNICEF

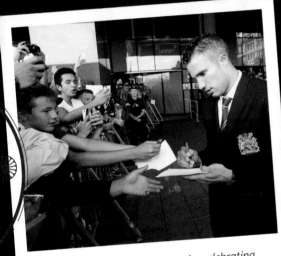

Birthday boy Robin van Persie, celebrating his 30th, meets the many fans outside the team hotel

STOCKHOLM

A host of big names made the journey to Sweden for the final tour match...

Match stats
Tuesday 6 August 2013, Friends Arena, Stockholm
AIK FOTBOLL 1 (Quaison 49)
MANCHESTER UNITED 1 (Henriquez 68)

The squad pose for a photo at the impressive Stockholm Stadium after a light work-out on the morning of the game

Angelo Henriquez enjoys a night to remember with a first United goal on his Reds debut

SPOT THE DIFFERENCE

Can you spot the 6 differences between the two celebration photographs?

Answers on page 60

WORDSEARCH

Hidden in the wordsearch below are 10 football-related words.
Can you find the words in the grid? Words can go horizontally,
vertically and diagonally in all eight directions.

L	P	H	R	D	L	U	O	F	C	E
N	M	E	K	J	L	S	L	K	O	T
K	J	T	N	Z	T	M	A	L	R	U
Y	E	K	E	A	Y	J	O	Q	N	T
N	T	N	D	E	L	N	G	W	E	I
C	K	I	X	Z	R	T	G	L	R	T
Q	U	Y	F	R	P	E	Y	G	H	S
M	R	R	L	J	P	K	F	C	R	B
T	N	W	L	T	L	R	T	E	T	U
H	V	T	Q	J	J	I	K	M	R	S
P	B	A	L	L	P	Y	F	R	Z	L

GOAL   **BALL**   **CORNER**   **FOUL**   **SUBSTITUTE**

NET   **PENALTY**   **STADIUM**   **REFEREE**   **PITCH**

Answers on page 60

RED REWIND

12 January 2008, United 6 Newcastle 0, Old Trafford

Barclays Premier League

The Reds hit Newcastle for six on a memorable day at Old Trafford, which also included Cristiano Ronaldo's one and only hat-trick for United, but what can you remember about the game?

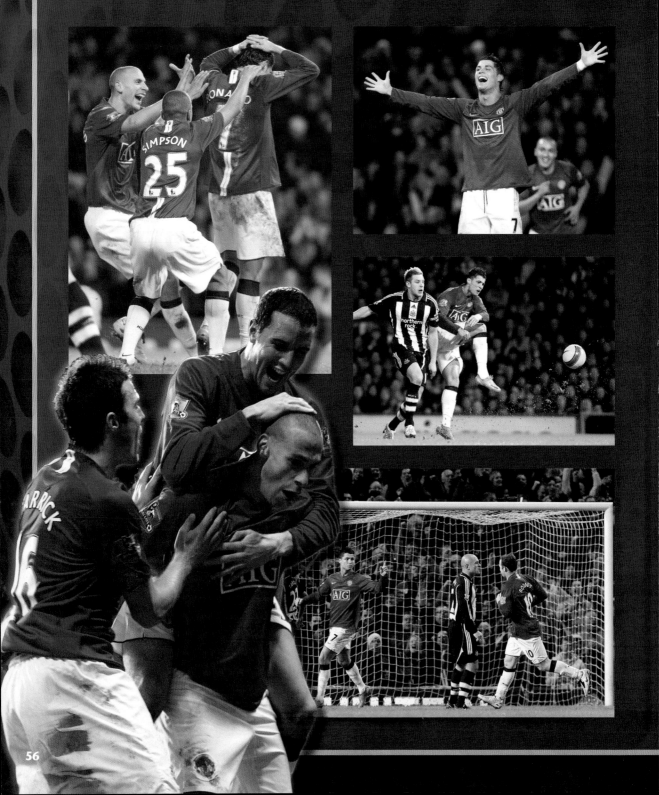

7:07 MANCHESTER UNITED **6**
NEWCASTLE UNITED **0** 0:00 MINS

1 In what minute did Ronaldo open the scoring – 47th, 49th or 51st?

2 Which defender also found the net on the day?

3 Who played in goal for the Reds?

4 Which former United player was sent off for Newcastle in injury-time?

5 Who took charge of Newcastle on the day?

Answers on page 61

GIGGS THE GREAT

He's been involved in an incredible 24 top flight seasons with the Reds and Ryan Giggs is still going strong. Can you guess which seasons the seven photos below of Ryan in action are from?

1.

2.

3.

4.

5.

6.

7.

Answers on page 61

TRUE OR FALSE

*Put your United knowledge to the test
with our Red teasers...*

1 **Chicharito scored United's last goal under
Sir Alex Ferguson before the Scot's retirement.**

2 **Rio Ferdinand once played in goal for United.**

3 **Robin van Persie scored 30 league goals during
the 2012/13 season.**

4 **Paul Scholes scored on his 700th appearance
for the Reds.**

5 **Ryan Giggs has scored over 100 goals in the
Premier League.**

6 **David Moyes used to manage Bristol City.**

ANAGRAMS

Unscramble the anagrams to reveal the names of six United stars...

1 Jigsaw Ha Akin

2 Bear Version Pin

3 Help Joins

4 Near Nods

5 Add Diva Gee

6 Shay Noel Guy

Answers on page 61

ANSWERS

Spot the Difference, Page 54

Wordsearch, Page 55

L	P	H	R	D	L	U	O	F	C	E
N	M	E	K	J	L	S	L	K	O	T
K	J	T	N	Z	T	M	A	L	R	U
Y	E	K	E	A	Y	J	O	Q	N	T
N	T	N	D	E	L	N	G	W	E	I
C	K	I	X	Z	R	T	G	L	R	T
Q	U	Y	F	R	P	E	Y	G	H	S
M	R	R	L	J	P	K	F	C	R	B
T	N	W	L	T	L	R	T	E	T	U
H	V	T	Q	J	J	I	K	M	R	S
P	B	A	L	L	P	Y	F	R	Z	L

Red Rewind, Pages 56-57

1 49th minute
2 Rio Ferdinand
3 Edwin van der Sar
4 Alan Smith
5 Nigel Pearson was caretaker boss following Sam Allardyce's departure three days before the match.

Giggs the Great, Page 58

1 2010-11
2 2007-08
3 2005-06
4 2012-13
5 2003-04
6 2002-03
7 1998-99

True or False, Page 59

1 TRUE – in the 5-5 draw at West Brom on 19 May 2013.
2 TRUE – he pulled on the gloves in United's FA Cup quarter-final defeat to Portsmouth at Old Trafford in March 2008 when substitute goalkeeper Tomasz Kuszczak was sent off.
3 FALSE – Robin scored 30 goals in total, but only 26 were in the league.
4 TRUE – Paul scored in his 700th game for United against Wigan on 15 September 2012.
5 TRUE – at the start of the 2013/14 season Ryan was on 109.
6 FALSE – David was a player at Bristol City, not a manager.

Anagrams, Page 59

1 Shinji Kagawa
2 Robin van Persie
3 Phil Jones
4 Anderson
5 David De Gea
6 Ashley Young

TROPHY HUNT

Can you find the Barclays Premier League trophy in this photo?